NATIONAL GEOGRAPHIC

I Like Apples

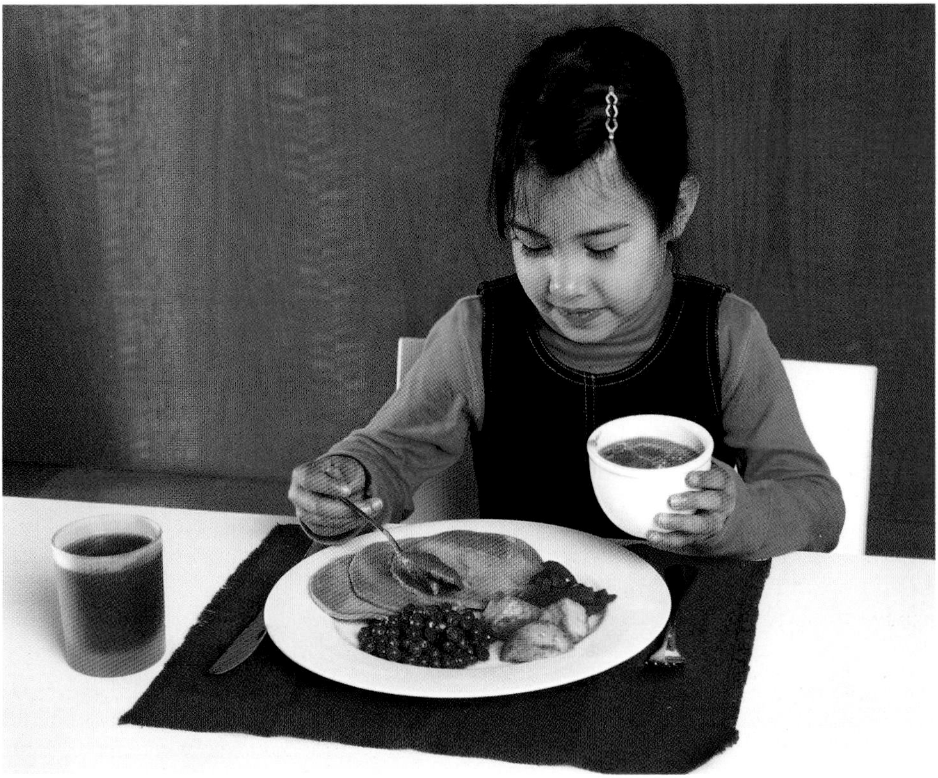

Karl Jensen

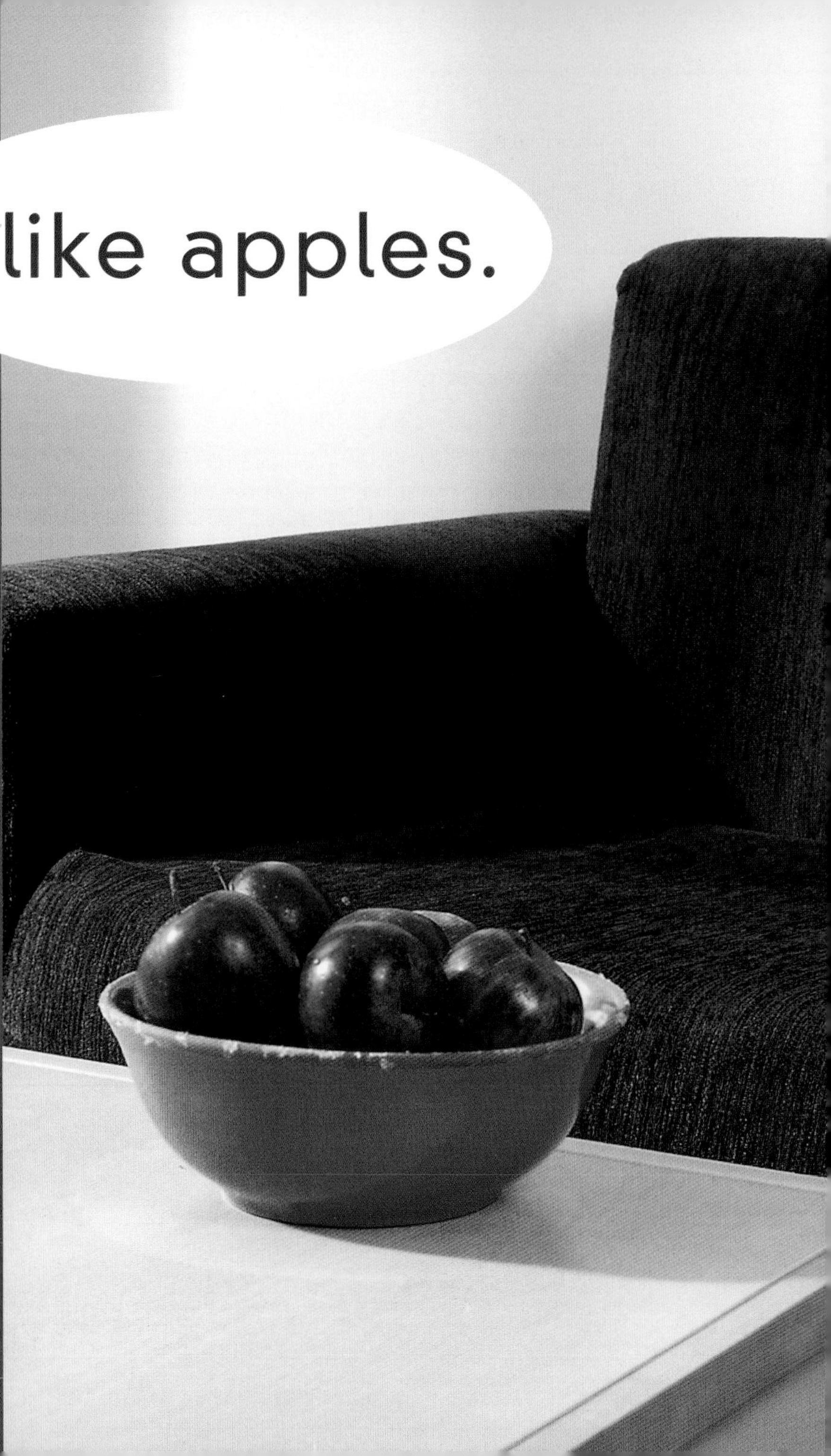
I like apples.

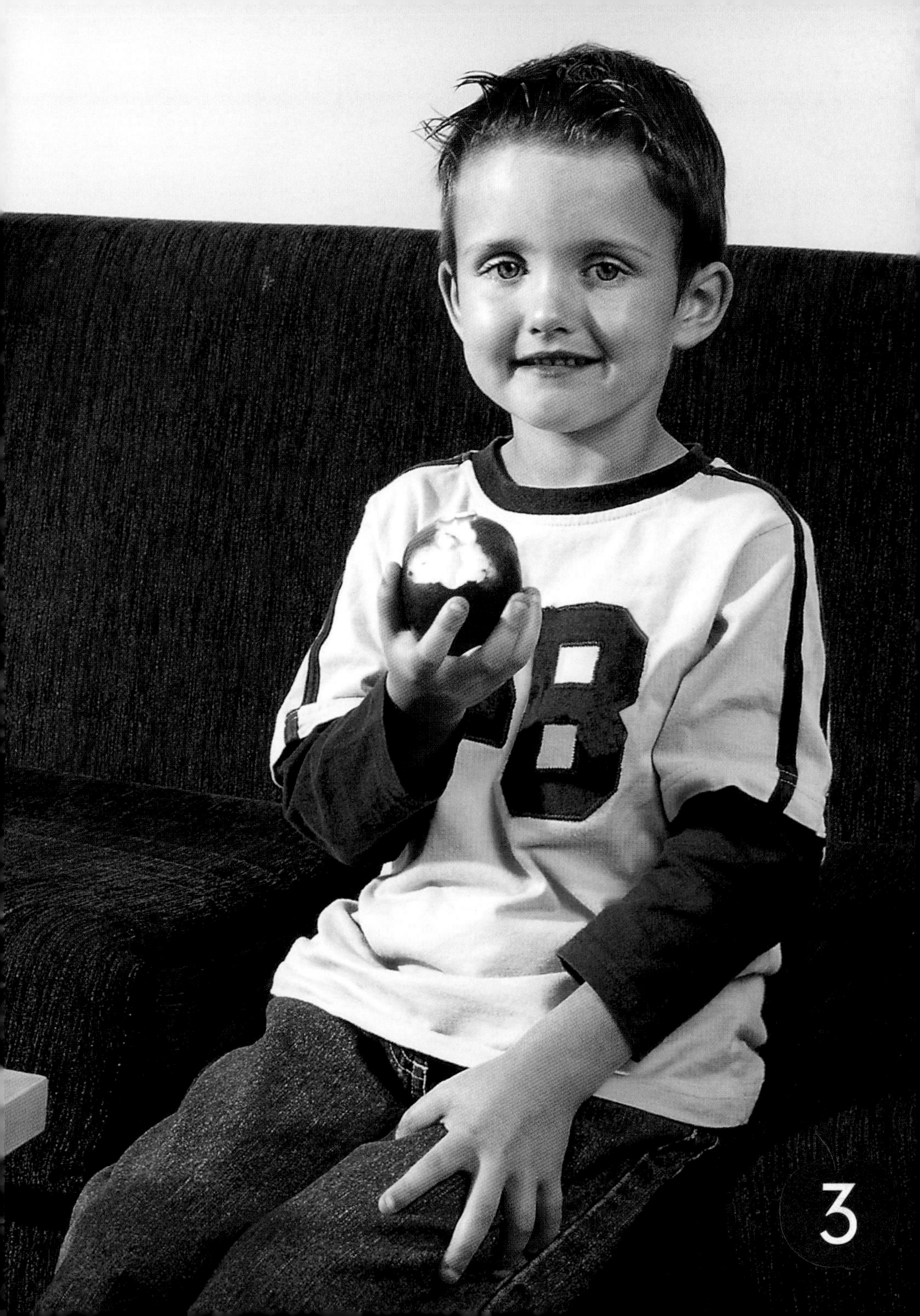

I like apples.

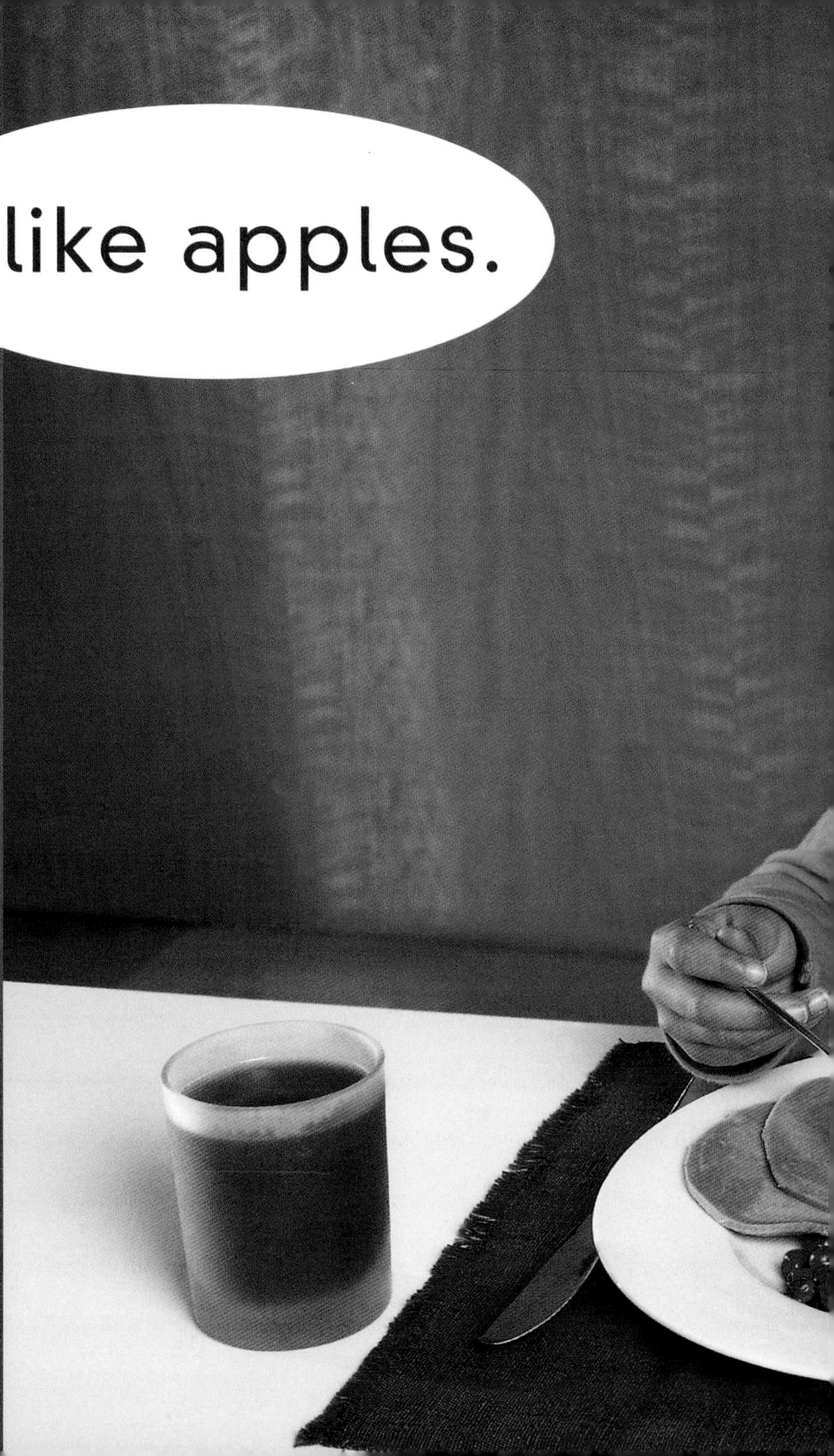

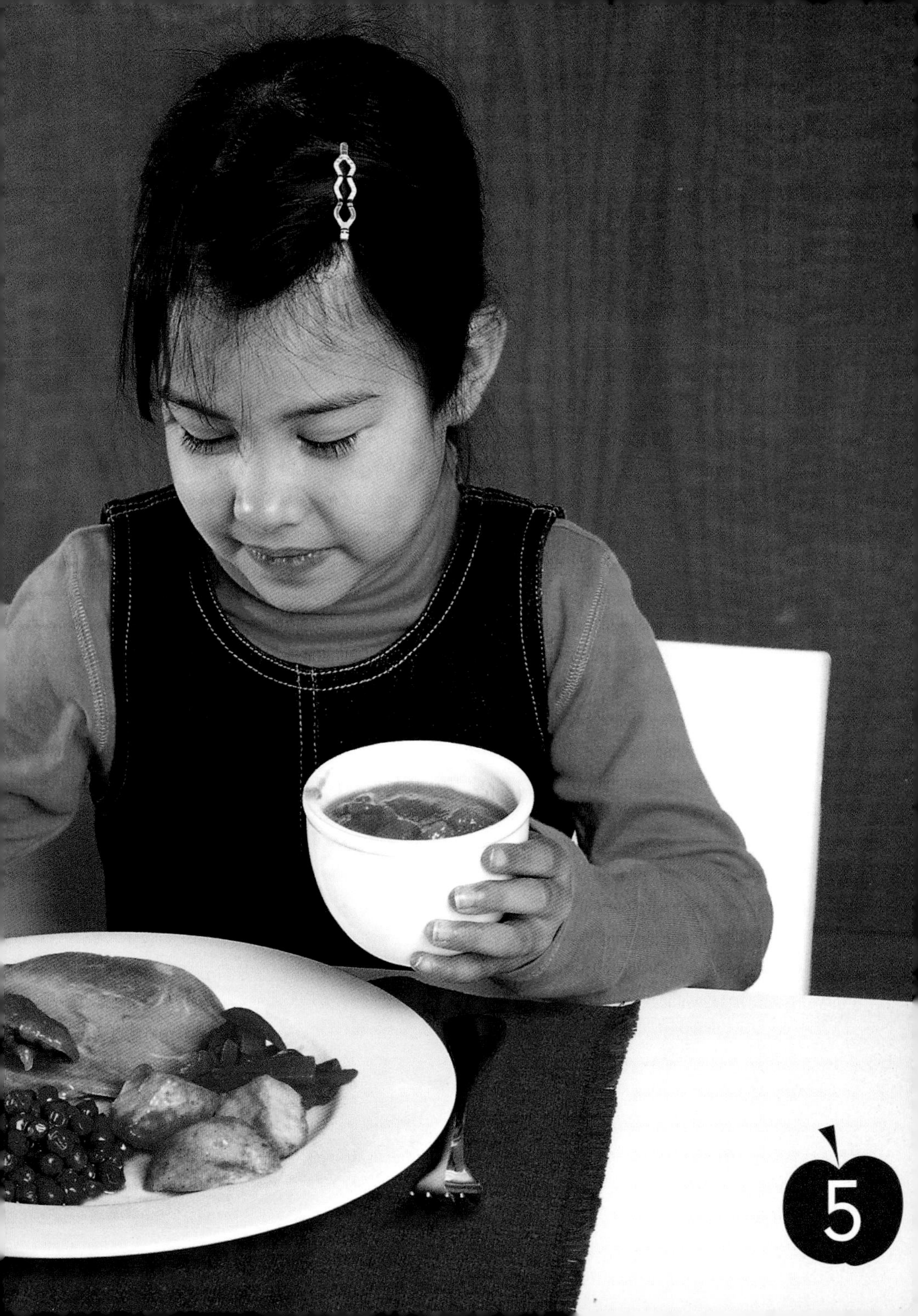

I like apples.

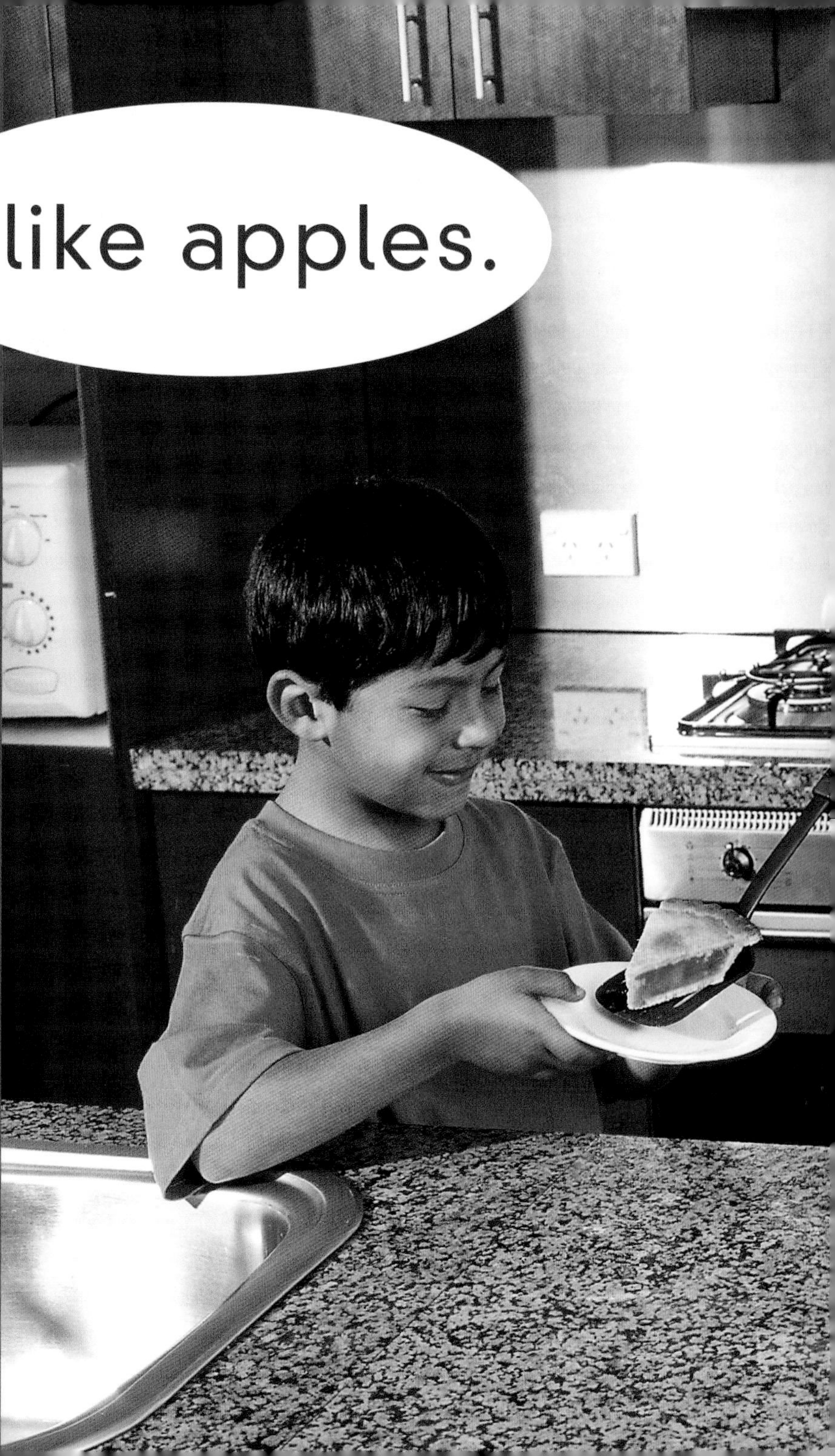

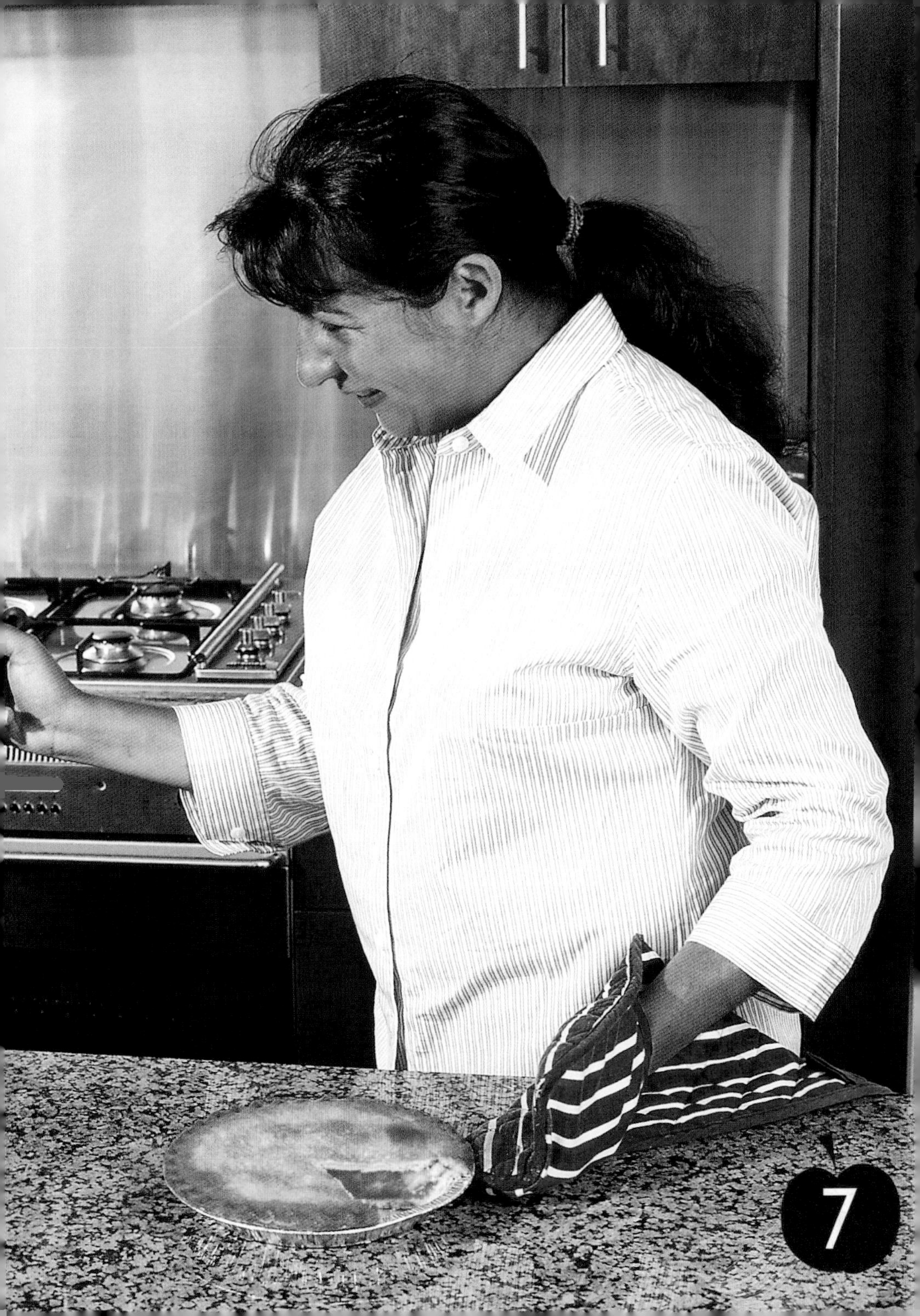

I like apples.

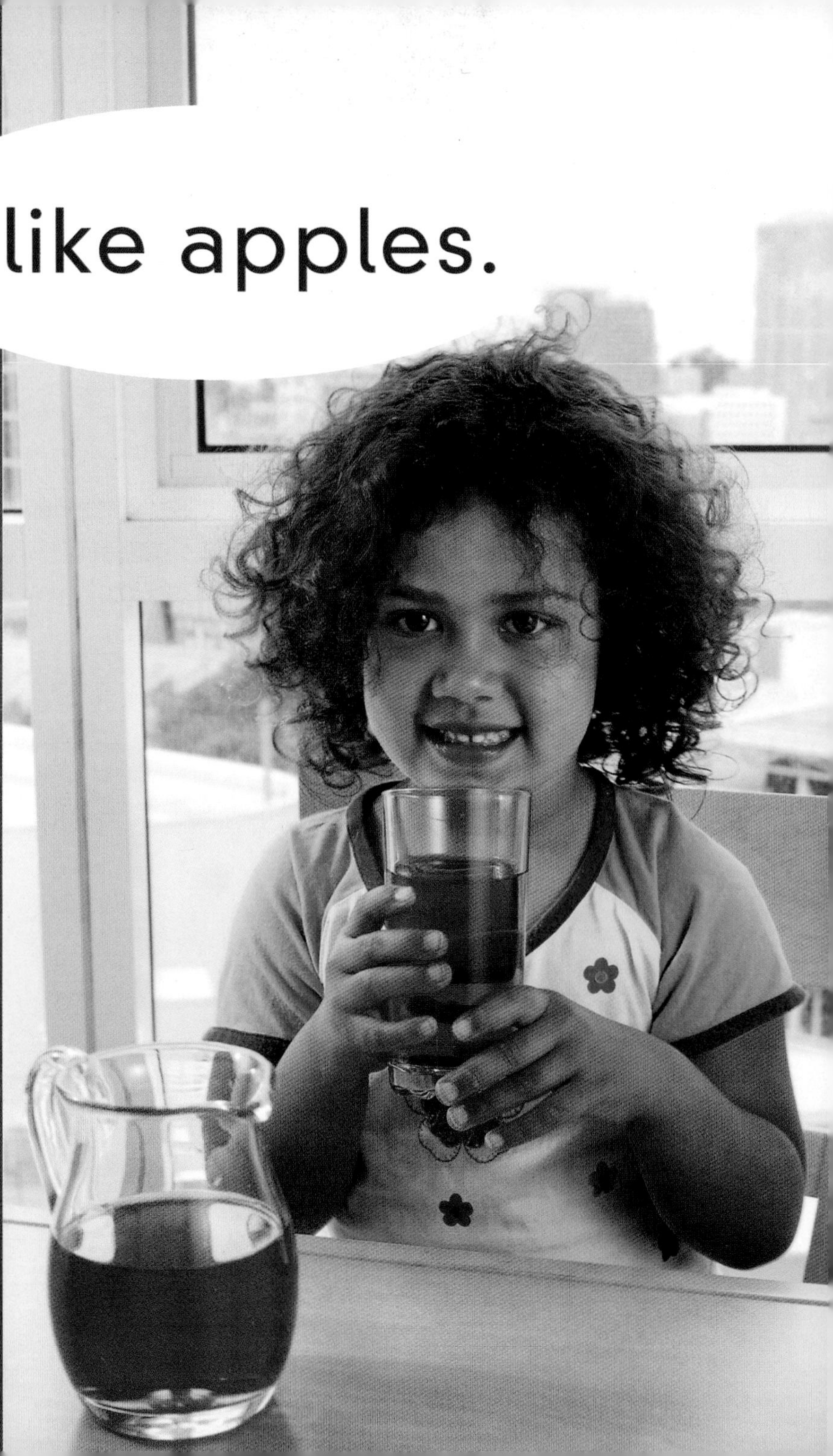